THE REAL ESTATE SURVIVAL GUIDE:
SECRETS, TIPS AND LIES FROM A BEVERLY HILLS SUPER AGENT

A GUIDE FOR HOMEBUYERS & SELLERS EVERYWHERE

BY KAREN NORRIS, REALTOR

NAMED "SUPER AGENT" BY LOS ANGELES MAGAZINE

KAREN NORRIS AND HER PASSION FOR PROVIDING REAL ESTATE ADVICE FOR THE NEW AND EXPERIENCED HOME BUYER AND SELLER

Karen Norris, a realtor with Coldwell Banker of Beverly Hills, has more than a dozen years experience in real estate, communications and marketing. She developed her business acumen in the trenches on Wall Street and understands how the financial markets affect homebuyers and sellers alike. Contract negotiations, marketing, innovative technology and a passion for client service are her most powerful assets.

In addition to traditional marketing, Karen offers her clientele the latest technologies and tools now available via the internet. One of the many services she offers is creating a secure website where her clients can review listings the second they come on the market. "Clients can now find a new home without wasting time driving around town to look at possible matches," she explains.

"I enjoy the personal touch to this business," she says. "Working with buyers and sellers on all aspects of the home-buying business can be rewarding on so many levels. Helping people find their dream home, or sell one as they move into another stage of life where their dreams have changed, is what being a realtor is all about."

Karen was recently named a **"SUPER AGENT"** by *Los Angeles Magazine*. Forty-two thousand ballots were mailed to *Los Angeles Magazine* subscribers asking them to nominate a top real estate professional with whom they had worked. More than three hundred surveys were also sent to top Los Angeles area real estate broker/managers asking them to nominate outstanding real estate agents who are superior in sales, integrity, market knowledge and who are an overall asset to the Los Angeles community.

The general survey and research process was designed to be comprehensive and to identify those real estate agents highly regarded by consumers as well as their professional peers. Credentials were scrutinized by a research team and points were assigned based upon defined evaluation criteria.

THE SECRETS OF BUYING A HOME   45

LIES ABOUT BUYING A HOME   49

WHEN IT COMES TO BUYING OR SELLING A HOME, IT'S NOT A BUYER'S MARKET OR A SELLER'S MARKET—
IT'S YOUR MARKET!

So much has been written about real estate by now that it's a testament to your courage as a buyer or seller that you've gotten this far. It says a lot about you, that you have slogged through dozens of aisles in the bookstore and have waded through endless titles on real estate to arrive at this particular title on this particular day. It bodes well for your search for a new home; or to find a buyer for your existing home. But that's what it takes in today's market – in any market – to succeed; relentless focus and courage.

There are few tasks as daunting as plunging into the real estate market for the first – or even the hundred and first – time. All those listings to visit, all of those tanks of gas you'll go through scouting out the neighborhoods, the schools, the shopping, the parking, the crowds.

There are movers to contact, calls to return, messages to leave, packing materials to cram into the trunk of your car and bubble wrap to engulf your most precious and fragile belongings.

There are strangers at your door with endless questions, trampling across your new carpet and wrinkling their noses over the children's artwork on the fridge.

Worse still, there is so much buzz surrounding the residential housing market these days, so many questions, it's hard to know *who* to believe, let alone *what.* Has the bubble burst? Are we on the rebound? Will prices drop? Should I buy now? Or wait? Is this the best time to sell? Trends generally go for three to five years in each direction and they can change at any time. This year's boom can be next year's bust.

The great humorist Mark Twain once said, "Buy land. They've quit making it." Truer words have never been spoken.

To buy or sell a home is to engage in one of the world's oldest practices. For centuries people have been buying and selling property; it is one of the truly universal activities we all share.

Of course, buying or selling a home today is a tad more complicated than it used to be. Trends, fads, bubbles, busts, speculators, investors, hucksters and email scams can all lead the frustrated home buyer or seller to throw their hands up in the air and quit the process altogether.

What you need is a guide; a helping hand. You might think that having your own realtor is enough. While it is true that you will need a realtor that is there for you, physically present, in real time, what about when you feel the need to ask a question at midnight? That's where this book comes in.

In addition to over a dozen years in the real estate business, I developed my business acumen in the trenches on Wall Street and consider contract negotiations, marketing, innovative technology and a passion for client service my most powerful assets.

Fair warning:

This book is not for speculators, investors, scam artists or grifters. I do not promise that your home will appreciate 400% over the next 3 months or that you'll be able to sell tomorrow for $100,000 more than you would have yesterday if you'll only follow my 10-easy steps, top-5 tips, 7 highly-effective strategies or 21 foolproof practices.

Trust me, with over a decade of experience in some of the most volatile and toughest markets on the planet, I can tell you that there's nothing "easy" or "foolproof" about real estate in *any* market.

That's still no reason why it can't be an enjoyable experience! The greatest thing about writing my own book based on my professional experience is that I can share valuable tips and secrets learned from some of the country's most successful realtors and industry thought leaders.

Why a book for buyers AND sellers? Why would buyers want to read what sellers have to go through and vice versa? Well, there's a perfectly good reason for that and it's called "knowing the other side's playbook." Now, don't get me wrong: I'm not one of these realtors that call one side the "good guys" and the other side the "bad guys." I build relationships between buyers and sellers because, quite frankly, it's an intimate one.

Consider this: As a buyer, you're going into people's homes, looking at their furniture, scrutinizing their tastes in wall colors and carpet shades, and generally taking over their private space for whatever time you're trampling their rugs or clomping up their stairs during an open house, walk through or go-see.

As a seller, you're not just letting people invade your private space; you're actually *inviting* them to do this! Now, if rooting through the closet of a complete stranger or flushing someone else's toilet upon your first meeting isn't intimate experiences, then I don't know what is!

And, this is all before the subject of money comes up; once it does, the gloves are usually off.

Well, I'm here to make the relationship between buyers and sellers a less combative one.

I believe that by understanding each other better, both buyers and sellers can have a more satisfying real estate experience.

Just because I work in Beverly Hills, don't let the zip code fool you. People in Beverly Hills, not to mention other high end markets around the country, have the same issues, concerns, strengths and weaknesses as people anywhere else. No matter what the budget is, the endgame is the same; get the most for your money.

Isn't that what real estate boils down to? We all want to get a good deal. Whether we're buying or selling, we want to feel that we haven't been swindled; that we've been treated fairly and professionally and at the end of the day – whether we're just moving in or turning over the keys to the front door – we want to look around, smile, and say, "This feels right."

Real estate, in general, and realtors, in particular, have gotten a bad rap lately. I'm here to change all that.

Buying or selling a home can be fun.

Sure, it's still a huge decision, a major shift in the financial ledgers, a gigantic step in some brand new direction, but that doesn't mean you can't enjoy the process along the way.

In all my years of helping clients buy and sell their homes, I have learned one universal truth: **Knowledge is power.** When you take the time to do your homework – as you're doing now by reading this book – when you take the time to gain that knowledge, you are invariably better prepared.

Knowledge is power.

It's true of buyers.

When you already know what to expect on your first open house, you're half as likely to make the simple mistakes that trip up so many home buyers these days.

Simply knowing what other houses are going for in the neighborhood, how old the home is, how many owners it has had or what new construction is planned for the neighborhood can better prepare you for an initial discussion with the seller.

Knowledge is power.

It's true of sellers. Understanding the rationale of a buyer, knowing the latest mortgage rates, talking to your neighbors who've had their "For Sale" sign up for six months. All of these simple strategies for gaining knowledge – and the dozens more I'll share with you in this book – give you the power to be a more knowledgeable seller.

Knowledge is power.

It's even true of realtors. Knowing what I do, doing what I do, keeping up with the professional journals, networking, hosting open houses every week, giving speeches at community events, hosting seminars, speaking to bankers, pricing similar homes in adjoining neighborhoods, satisfying clients and following-up on recent sales, all of these tools enable me to have more knowledge of the local market and, as a result, more power for my clients.

Knowledge is power.

And by the end of this book, it will be true of you.

PART 1
SELLING
TIPS, SECRETS & LIES
WHEN SELLING A HOME

TIPS FOR SELLING A HOME

"You should have sold last year" are words that homeowners hate to hear. The best kept secret in real estate isn't what to buy or even when to buy. The greatest secret is knowing when to sell. Selling into a strong market where there is a lot of demand is not only the way to maximize profits; it is also the easiest time to sell a piece of property. Because real estate is not a liquid asset you would rather be out of the market wanting in than in the market wanting out. This chapter provides many "insider" tips on selling a home.

TOP 5 MARKET CONDITIONS
THAT ARE IDEAL FOR SELLING A HOME

1. Home sale activity is strong and the number of houses on the market is declining.
2. The economy is strong and unemployment is low.
3. New home construction is on the rise.
4. Mortgage rates are low and financing is easy to obtain.
5. Consumer confidence is high and media reports are optimistic about the economy.

MARKETING STRATEGIES THAT SELL

There are a variety of marketing strategies that you and your agent (if you choose to work with one) can launch. They include:

PRICE IT RIGHT: Perform a *Comparative Market Analysis* **(CMA)** of recent listings and sales in your area to determine your selling price. This is the single most important task to prepare your property for sale. Resist the temptation to overprice your property by even $10,000 or $20,000 because it can ending up costing you much more later.

MLS: List your property on the local MLS (The Multiple Listing Service is only available through member real estate agents) to reach thousands of agents and buyers immediately. Remember to display at least 6 photos.

Industry statistics have shown that 6 is the magic number because it allows viewers to get a better sense of the layout, feel and flow of the property.

WWW: List your property on the internet on sites such as www.Realtor.com, www.Homestore.com, www.Homeseekers.com www.ForSaleByOwner.com. If you work with a professional realtor, your listing will automatically appear on www.Realtor.com.

TWILIGHT OPEN HOUSES: Many houses look softer and prettier at night, and in some cases it's an opportunity to showcase a city light view or romantic sunset.

THE TALKING HOUSE: See www.talkinghouse.com. A radio-transmitter broadcasts a sales message from you 24/7 over the airwaves. House hunters tune their car radios to get the details about your property.

NEWSPAPER ADVERTISING: Old-fashioned? Yes. Effective? Absolutely!

PROPER POSTAGE REQUIRED: You or your real estate agent should send out "*Just Listed*" postcards to all homeowners in the area. You or your realtor can get names and addresses from the local title company.

OPEN HOUSES: Hold "Broker's only" Open Houses on Tuesdays to allow all of the local realtors to preview the property.

Host Saturday and Sunday Open Houses from 1 to 4 PM for the public.

IN-BOX ETIQUETTE: If you are working with an agent, broadcast an email flyer to all brokers in the area.

PROS & CONS OF HIRING AN AGENT
PROS

1) UP-TO-THE MINUTE STATISTICS ON COMPETING PROPERTIES – These are key facts at an agent's fingertips that can get immediate action on your property.

2) MARKETING TO OTHER REAL ESTATE AGENTS AND PROSPECTIVE BUYERS – Your agent has the resources and experience to market your property to other real estate agents locally, as well as worldwide, if necessary. They can disburse information about your property to other real estate agents through targeted Multiple Listing Services and many other cooperative marketing networks and relocation companies. They will also host all of your Open Houses.

3) GATEKEEPERS – Real Estate agents are like your surrogate and gatekeeper. They sit on the frontlines and act on your behalf. They will pre-screen, accompany and answer all questions for prospects.

4) LEGAL COUNSEL – Since your agent works for a broker, you have access to a wealth of legal advice and counsel and, for the most part, it's all FREE.

5) PRESENT OFFERS – Your agent will help you screen for the best-qualified buyers and assist you in evaluating offers as well as negotiating the terms and conditions.

6) OVERCOMING OBSTACLES – Between the initial sales agreement and closing, obstacles or issues often arise. Examples include; an unexpected repair, issues with the title, a judgment or tax lien is identified, etc. The required paperwork to resolve many of these issues are overwhelming for most sellers. Your agent has the experience to handle each smoothly and professionally.

CONS

1) COMMISSION CONCERNS – A broker generally charges a commission of 5 to 6% of the sales price for brokering a property. These costs cover exposure to the substantial legal risks and liabilities involved in brokering a property, mounds of paperwork, legwork, marketing and advertising.

SETTING THE STAGE INSIDE & OUT

It is important that your house "look the part." To ensure maximum positive exposure, be sure to pay close attention to both of the following zones:

INSIDE – remove all clutter, family photos (which are a distraction), clean and paint walls (or at least touch them up) and steam clean carpeting. I suggest that you leave the lighting fixtures and drapes in place – even if they are not included in the sale – because they add character.

OUTSIDE – have your address number repainted on the curb, touchup paint on house gutters and mailbox, remove toys, clutter and trash, have the walkway stairs re-painted, polish front light fixtures and replace bulbs, plant flowers and place pots by front entrance.

NO SELLERS ALLOWED

It's nothing personal, but sellers can be a distraction during a showing or Open Houses. You may think you're being helpful by being around to answer questions or point out an attractive feature, but think about how you feel when aggressive salespeople stalk you on the showroom floor. Let the buyers have the freedom to roam the property, speak freely and visualize their life and belongings in your environment. Sometimes they are hesitant to do this if the sellers are around.

CATS & DOGS ARE OUT, TOO!

Sellers, you're in good company! Since many folks are plagued with pet allergies and dogs love to bark at strangers and cats love to wind around legs of the unsuspecting guests, the house should be pet-free during open houses and showings. The mission is to keep distractions to a minimum so the buyers can focus on what *really* matters to them.

PRE-MARKET INSPECTION

Even with full disclosure laws enforced nationwide, there are some who would prefer to subscribe to the *"Don't Know, Don't Tell"* policy. Translation: If sellers are unaware of defects in the home they do not have to disclose it. Since a smart buyer will hire their own general inspector to fully inspect your home anyway, it is better to have prior knowledge on what they might find so you can make the repairs ahead of time or be prepared when the buyer negotiates repairs into the price.

WHEN YOU'RE HOT, *YOU'RE HOT!*
WHEN YOU'RE NOT – *WHAT'S NEXT?*

Timing is everything. Translation: A house is never hotter than in the first 2-3 weeks it hits the market. If you've been careful to price it accurately and have implemented strong marketing strategies and don't see a lot of activity during that initial marketing window, you could be experiencing a shift in the market. Here is a quick way to tell:
- Low attendance at Open Houses (5 people or less).
  - 5-10 showings with no offers.
  - Well priced home on the market 30 days or longer.

SOLUTION: Take the property off the market for at least 30 days and re-enter the market with a significant price reduction. This is usually enough to "prime the pump" and affect a dramatic change in activity.

THE OFFERS ARE IN...
WHICH ONE SHOULD I CHOOSE?

Multiple offers are a seller's dream. Have your agent list them on a work-sheet outlining the strengths and weaknesses of each one. This is key. It's important to evaluate each offer on a variety of pros and cons, and not just the highest offer – or closest to your listing price. This way, you can counter and negotiate each one separately or respond to all of them with a "Request for Highest & Best Offer."

Here's what to look for:

- The offer closest to the asking price.
- Buyers who are **pre-approved** for a loan.
- Few or no contingencies. These are possible occurrences that could release them from the contract, such as inspections or the inability to sell their home first or obtain financing.
- Competitive earnest money deposit and down payment.
- 30 day or less escrow period.

THE ROAD THROUGH ESCROW BEGINS

An escrow agent is a neutral third party whom the buyer and seller agree upon to carry out all closing instructions. They assume responsibility for processing all of the required paperwork and final distribution of funds.

The escrow process begins when the buyer-signed "Offer to Purchase" has been accepted and signed by the seller.

SIGNED SEALED & DELIVERED –
OFFER ACCEPTED:
PROCEED WITH CAUTION

You have accepted an offer and escrow has been opened. It is important to note that nearly 50% of all escrows fall through, which is why, when there are multiple offers, I recommend placing the original 2nd Choice Offer in 1st backup position.

It might take a day or two for the buyers who were beaten out to accept a secondary backup position, but if they really loved the property, they'll jump on board. Your agent will handle the paperwork, officially placing them in the "First Backup Position."

LET THE INSPECTIONS BEGIN –
FEAR IS NOT A FACTOR IN THIS GAME

The next step is to allow the buyers to perform all requested and necessary inspections and to disclose all known defects or issues regarding the property. Normal inspection periods are outlined in the offer and usually completed within a 7-day period.

You can count on the fact that something unexpected will surface during this process, but remember that **EVERYTHING** can be negotiated. Here is what to expect:

- Termite Inspection
- General Physical Inspection
- Mold Inspection (if the general inspection sites danger zones)
- Appraisal of the property and possibly a land survey
- Natural Hazard Inspection that will disclose if the property is in a flood zone, fire zone, earthquake fault zone, seismic hazard zone hurricane area or wild land area that may contain substantial forest fire risks and hazards.
- State government mandated retrofitting, which varies from city to city and includes inspections to see that low flow toilets are installed, water heaters are strapped, earthquake shut-off valves are in place and smoke detectors are functioning properly.
- Additional inspections that you might want to have performed include asbestos and radon testing.
- Buyers might also ask for copies of utility bills to get a sense of the costs.

AND THE JOURNEY THROUGH ESCROW CONTINUES...

Be forewarned that the escrow process is typically a long (30 to 45 days) and tedious one. Here are some of the activities that take place during escrow:

- A title insurance company conducts a title search to determine, among other things, whether the seller will be able to transfer a clean marketable title, free of liens and encumbrances to the buyer.
- The escrow company obtains demand statements from lenders and other creditors to be paid off before the escrow closes.
- The escrow company may obtain loan documents and instructions from the buyer's lender for the buyer to sign.
- The escrow company figures tax and interest pro-rations, prepares the closing paperwork and arranges for the buyers and sellers to sign the closing paperwork.
- Homeowner's Association documents are requested by the escrow company and reviewed and approved by the buyers.
- The buyers conduct a final "walk-through" of the property to confirm that the home is in the same condition as when the offer was accepted and that any agreed upon repairs have been completed satisfactorily.
- After signatures are obtained from the buyers, the loan documents are sent back to the lender for funding.
- The escrow company records the necessary documents in the new buyer's names with the county where the property is located, thereby closing the transaction.
- The escrow company disburses the appropriate funds and sends copies of the closing paperwork to the appropriate parties.
  Congratulations! The buyer can now pickup the keys and move in.

MORE TIPS FOR THE SELLER

Finally, here are a few additional tips that will help to guide you through the sales process:

- Have a floor plan of your home available for prospective buyers to take with them.
- Buyers pay extra attention to your roof, so replace missing shingles or tiles, repair and paint eaves and clean gutters.

Since the kitchen is the most important room to buyers, here is a checklist of things to do:
- Clean and inspect all appliances and make sure they work properly.
- Replace cabinet knobs if necessary.
- Check leaks in kitchen plumbing and repair any problems.
- Clean all tile grout.
- Re-caulk kitchen sink.
- Organize kitchen cabinets.
- Touch up paint.
- If cabinets are in poor condition replace the fronts.
- Clean and polish hardwood floors.

THE SECRETS OF SELLING A HOME

Secrets. They are part and parcel of a realtor's skill at cutting to the chase. The more secrets we know the better. Why? Because we're all the more prepared to avoid the future harm such unknown secrets can deliver. Here is what you need to know:

BROKER/AGENT NOT PERFORMING? YOU'RE FIRED!

Even though you've signed a standard 3 to 6 month Exclusive Listing Agreement with your broker, you have the right to terminate the contract anytime you feel you are not being represented well. Write a letter to the broker expressing your dissatisfaction and indicate that you wish to cancel the agreement. Ninety-nine per cent of the time they will release you from the contract without incident. What about the other one-percent? To make it "bullet-proof," incorporate a "Cancellation Clause" into your Listing Agreement indicating that you have the right to cancel at anytime for non-performance by the Agent.

STAY IN YOUR HOME FOR THE HOLIDAYS

Ho-Ho-NO! No matter what you've heard in the past, holidays are the *worst* time of year to put your home on the market. Here are some reasons why:
- People are distracted with many activities over the holidays and not in the mindset of buying a home.
- Many buyers who are out at this time are bottom-feeders that like to make low ball offers and have been doing so all year long, merely waiting for the perfect opportunity to find a desperate seller.
- Most people travel this time of year and attendance at Open Houses is very low. People who put their homes on the market over the holidays are perceived as "desperate" in the marketplace.

"MUM" IS THE WORD

Resist the temptation to enter into a "friendly conversation" with your buyers before closing. Every word you say can and will be held against you in a court of law. MUM is also the word when the buyers ask why you are moving. If they detect an urgent need to move they will attempt to offer a lower price. A good response to why you are moving is simply, "The time is right and we will move if we receive the price we are looking for."

OOPS -WE PRICED IT TOO LOW

Although the research and due-diligence suggested that you were on target with the selling price, should you be lucky enough to receive multiple offers *over* the asking price, there is a strong possibility that you have undervalued your property. Sit down with your agent, study the offers carefully and consider re-listing the property with an increased purchase price. Remember, you are never obligated to sell your home to even the highest bidder.

BEWARE OF HIRING FRIENDS AND RELATIVES AS YOUR AGENT

Selling a home is one of the most important financial decisions you will make and will most likely be an emotional roller coaster. The skills needed to sell your home for the most money and ensure the transaction goes smoothly are gained through years of education and experience.

Hire family and friends to represent you at your own peril! Not choosing a professional with a strong track record to represent you can cost you money, frustration and stress. Due to the intense negotiations and emotional volatility involved in the process, it is best to work with a professional agent with whom you are emotionally unattached.

NOT ALWAYS ABOUT THE MONEY

It's not always about the money. In fact, most people buy homes based on emotion. The more you appeal to a buyer's emotions during the negotiation process, the less money is an issue.

IS THERE A PRE-PAYMENT PENALTY IN YOUR MORTGAGE?

When is the early bird putting her neck out too far? Many sellers get to the closing date and find out they have a several thousand dollar prepayment penalty fee for paying off their mortgage early. Contact your lender to review the terms of the loan before putting your home on the market.

IS YOUR EX'S NAME STILL ON THE TITLE?

If there is any doubt about a clear title on your property, the time to clean it up is *before* you put it on the market, not after.

In the case of divorce, if the ex's name still appears on the title you will need to get the ex to sign a "Quitclaim Deed" to the property.

An attorney or escrow company can handle this for you.

HIDDEN DANGERS IN NEW LANDSCAPING PROJECTS

Use extreme caution when digging up and moving soil around to create interesting landscaping effects, especially when adding new trees and shrubs. Any grading or changing of the natural landscape done without the consultation of a geologist may impact the flow of water during a rain, possibly resulting in water runoff onto your neighbor's property. Removing or adding trees and shrubs may change the natural flow of water during a rain.

To avoid a lawsuit when selling your home, be sure to disclose the extent of your landscaping work to the buyer and whether or not you consulted with a professional geologist or landscaper.

LIES ABOUT SELLING A HOME

One of my favorite parts about writing this book was the ability to shed light on some of my favorite – or should I say "least favorite" – lies concerning selling a home. I hope by shedding the light on these scurrilous issues that you'll be better prepared than the average home seller to avoid them.

YOU HAVE 3 FULL PRICE OFFERS... YOU ARE OBLIGATED TO SELL

Selling your home is a huge decision. Whose decision is it? Yours and yours alone. Don't ever allow anyone to force you into selling your home. Even if you have 5 written offers on your property that are over the asking price, you are not obligated to accept any of them. Many brokers will strong-arm their clients into accepting an offer… don't do it unless you are happy with *all* of the terms. You are not obligated to sell until you have accepted and signed the Purchase Offer and the buyers have been notified of the acceptance.

MORE IS BETTER: MAKE ALL THE IMPROVEMENTS YOU WANT

Many people think that "more is better" when making improvements to a home. Not so. In fact, sometimes "less is more." You must exercise caution when remodeling and ensure that the upgrades are consistent with what the neighborhood can support. Checkout Open Houses in your neighborhood and examine at what level improvements have been made. You might want to save those imported tiles, slate roof and Koi pond until you move into an area where you'll get a worthwhile return on your investment.

NO BUYER WANTS TO WAIT UNTIL YOU SELL YOUR HOME

Do not make the mistake of putting your home on the market "subject to" your finding another home. It's a waste of time and will discourage serious buyers from considering your home. Buyers won't want to wait around for you to find another home. These days, with extended stay motels and reasonably-priced storage, you can feel confident that you won't be sleeping on the curb!

YOUR SELLING PRICE MUST BE DISCLOSED IN PUBLIC RECORDS

False. In most states, you may keep the selling price of your property confidential. Depending on the state, for a fee of approximately $250 the escrow company will fill out the necessary paperwork to keep the selling price out of public records and The Multiple Listing Service.

SELLING "AS IS" EXEMPTS YOU FROM FULL DISCLOSURE

Don't make the mistake of thinking that selling in "As Is" condition makes you exempt from full disclosure. It simply does not work and you can get sued. Ask the buyers to take the property in "As Is" condition, but only after you have disclosed all the problems and they know what they are getting. In this section I am *disclosing* lies in real estate; not encouraging them!

A MURDER OR DEATH IN THE HOUSE CAN BE OUR SECRET

Not a chance. The consequences could be severe if a seller does not disclose this information. Anything and everything that could materially affect the desirability of the property – and a murder on property is a biggie – must be disclosed. Anything less would be duplicitous.

YOUR OFFER IS ACCEPTED... THE MARKETING IS OVER

Most buyers will try to persuade the sellers to stop showing the property and discontinue holding Open Houses after their offer has been accepted. Under no circumstances should the seller stop marketing the property until the inspection periods are over and all contingencies have been removed.

I MUST USE THE MONEY FROM MY HOME SALE TO BUY ANOTHER PROPERTY

This used to be the only way to get around a tax bill on a home sale. Even then, you were only able to defer taxes by purchasing a new residence of equal or greater value with the profits from your other house. When you sold your final house, you'd owe those long-deferred taxes you had rolled over throughout the years. Home sellers age 55 or older were allowed an once-in-a-lifetime tax exemption of up to $125,000 in sale profit.

But, on May 7, 1997, the home-sale tax law changed. Now, if you live in the house for two of the five years before you sell, the IRS won't collect tax on sale profit of up to $250,000 if you're single or $500,000 if you and your spouse file a joint return.

SOMETIMES YOUR FRIENDLY NEIGHBOR GETS DRUNK AND SHOOTS HIS GUN BUT EVERYBODY LOVES HIM ANYWAY... NO BIG DEAL.

False. It is a big deal! Let's say you own a home in a quiet and peaceful neighborhood, but there is a neighbor down the street who has a habit of yelling and occasionally shooting his gun into the air when he gets drunk on the weekends. Even though everybody loves him, he can get you sued if you sell your home without disclosing that information.

Your neighbor may not disturb you, but your neighbor's weekend habits are deemed a *material fact* requiring disclosure *in writing* to your buyer.

NOTES

PART 2
BUYING
TIPS, SECRETS & LIES
WHEN BUYING A HOME

TIPS FOR BUYING A HOME

Buyers, this section is for you. In this section I have included a distillation of over a dozen years in the industry creating satisfied home buyers, one "welcome" mat at a time! Remember my motto: It's not a buyer's or a seller's market; it's YOUR market. These tips will help guide you through it:

FIRST THINGS FIRST: GET THAT CREDIT IN SHAPE

Contact a credit bureau or check the internet for a credit report on yourself. If you don't like what you see, at least you will have time to clean up any problem items. Here are some ways to do just that:

- If possible, reduce your credit card debt by paying down balances.
- Take an inventory of your finances and determine the price you can afford to pay for a home and how much you want to spend.
- Research mortgage rates and terms on the internet (see websites at the back of this book).
- Get pre-approved for a loan. Obtaining loan pre-approval will help you in two ways: first, it will impress a seller and, second, it can usually increase your chances of negotiating a good price. Make an appointment with a mortgage banker and determine what type of a mortgage will work best for you. Find out how much down payment is required, both the interest rate and the Annual Percentage Rate (APR), standard closing costs and any extra fees the lender may charge.

RESEARCH MARKET CONDITIONS IN THE AREA

Buying a home when the real estate market is depressed and when there are an abundance of properties on the market can always yield the greatest profits. When property values are depressed and the media is full of dismal news, the stage is set for the next real estate uptrend. These are the top 5 market indicators that describe a depressed real estate market which is also the best time to buy:

1. Home sale activity is low. There are few buyers and an abundance of homes on the market.
2. Construction activity is down and few new building permits are being issued.
3. The economy is sluggish and unemployment is high.
4 Foreclosures are high and mortgage financing is more difficult to get. Both mortgage rates and interest rates are high.
5. Consumer confidence is low and media reports are dismal.

To help you determine whether it's a Buyer's Market or Seller's Market, here are some clear-cut definitions:

- A **buyer's market** exists when there is an abundance of properties for sale, and the timeframe to sell the properties is lengthy.
- A **seller's market** exists when there is a shortage of properties for sale and homes sell quickly (less than 30 days).

To find properties for sale and to see how long they have been on the market go to http://www.realtor.com. To obtain information about regional market conditions and statistics go to http://www.DQNews.com.

GET EXCITED ABOUT THE PROCESS AND DO SOME DETECTIVE WORK

The process can begin as soon as you think you might want to become a new homeowner. Begin combing the classified ads in the real estate section of your newspaper, visit open houses, tour new home communities on weekends, and search the internet for homes. This will help you determine the price-range and neighborhood you would like to live in.

THE PROS & CONS OF HIRING AN AGENT

PROS

1) DETERMINE YOUR BUYING POWER – An agent can help you determine your financial reserves, as well as your borrowing capacity. An agent can also refer you to those lenders best qualified to help you.

2) PRIVATE LISTINGS – Sometimes the property you are seeking is available but not actively advertised in the marketplace. By networking with other agents and being on the frontline, working open houses, an agent has a vast amount of resources available to help identify private listings.

3) COMMUNITY RESOURCES – Agents have access to a variety of informational resources and can provide local community information on utilities, zoning and schools, as well as other critically important and relevant facts about an area.

4) NEGOTIATIONS – There are a myriad of negotiating factors, including price, financing, terms, date of possession, inclusion or exclusion of repairs and furnishings or equipment. The Purchase Agreement should provide a period of time for you to complete appropriate inspections and investigations of the property before you are bound to complete the purchase. Your agent can advise you as to which investigations and inspections are recommended or required.

5) EVALUATION OF THE PROPERTY – Depending on the area, this includes inspections for termites, dry rot, asbestos, faulty structure, roof condition, just to name a few. Your agent can assist you in finding qualified, responsible professionals to do most of these investigations and provide you with written reports. You will also want to see a preliminary report on the title of the property. Your agent can help you identify and resolve title issues that might cause problems at a later date.

6) CLOSING – There will be an enormous amount of paperwork to review and sign. Your agent can guide you step by step through the closing process and make sure you have a thorough understanding of all of the documents.

7) ONGOING COUNSEL – After the sale there are always issues that surface and your agent will be there, ready to help. They can also give you periodic updates on market conditions to keep you informed about the status of your investment.

CONS

1) FEES – A buyer pays no fee to a real estate agent because the buyer's commission is paid by the seller. The seller incorporates this fee into the selling price of the property.   Therefore, a buyer has absolutely nothing to lose – and everything to gain – by being represented by an agent. The only possible exemption is when a buyer buys directly from the seller or the seller's agent. In this case, the seller will occasionally reduce the price. Remember that being represented by the seller's agent may provide an economic advantage but does not necessarily ensure objective representation for the buyer.

THE HOME IS NOT ONLY ABOUT LIFESTYLE... THINK "INVESTMENT"

When buying a home we generally think about comfort and lifestyle for ourselves. Cozy, yes, but think again. Your home is one of the largest purchases you will ever make, so it pays to also view it as a long-term investment. Some things to consider:
- Convenience to work and schools.
- Proximity to parks, gyms, fire stations, police stations, hospitals, airports, restaurants, shopping centers.
- Growth/expansion potential.
- CC & R's (Conditions, Covenants and Requirements).
- Neighborhood should be renovating and on the upswing.
- Should have features appealing to the next buyers.

- Future plans for the neighborhood and surrounding area.
- Research the zoning laws for the area.
- Property taxes and special assessments
- Homeowner's insurance (including special coverage such as flood zones, earthquake, etc.)
- In the case of condominiums – association dues, restrictions, etc.

JUST DO IT: HIRE A REAL ESTATE AGENT

Hiring a good local agent will eliminate an enormous amount of stress and add extreme value in the home buying process. Many homebuyers think that when you hire a real estate agent you must pay them a fee. NOT TRUE. *The buyers do not pay a fee.* The sellers incorporate the commissions into the selling price and the commissions are paid to the real estate agent at the close of escrow by the seller.

Need more convincing? Recently, The National Association of Realtors conducted a nationwide search of Homebuyers and Sellers to determine how they ranked resources available to them. Here is what they found:

Real estate agents	86%
Yard signs	69%
Internet	65%
Newspaper	49%
Magazines	35%
Open Houses	48%
Builders	37%
Television	22%

DO YOUR HOMEWORK ON
RECENT SALES IN THE AREA

How do you stack up? Ask your agent to do a **Comparative Market Analysis** (CMA). This will provide you with a list of all of the comparable properties that have sold within the last 6 months in the neighborhood where you are looking to buy.

Also get a list of those neighborhood homes currently on the market.

Comparables, in fact, are the principal tool brokers and appraisers themselves use to appraise property for market value. Other considerations in making price comparisons include the condition of the house, size of the property, time of year, special financing available, and the general economic climate – whether it's a buyer's or seller's market.

BECOME A SPY AND CASE THE NEIGHBORHOOD

You test drive a car before you buy it, right? Why should buying a house be any different? Drive, bike or walk through a community at different times of the day to get a feeling for the community. Here are some quick tips on the When & Why:

- In the morning, when people are going to school and work.
- During the day, to checkout renovations and lawn maintenance.
- At night, to check on parking, noise and lighting.
- Is the neighborhood dog friendly? Too dog friendly?
- Talk to as many neighbors as you can…they are a great resource and will usually tell you everything.

21 TIPS TO CONSIDER WHEN ATTENDING AN OPEN HOUSE

1. This is where the real work begins. Take this list with you when you head out to preview all of those properties:
2. Take a digital camera with you (always ask before taking photos).
3. Take a tape measure.
4. Does the home have good curb appeal? Does it draw you in?
5. When you enter the front door does it have an open feeling?

6. Does the home smell of tobacco, pets, dampness?

7. What kind of natural light exists? Too much? Not enough?

8. Lift area rugs to inspect floors underneath.

9. Any water stains on the ceiling or floors?

10. Are the floors in good condition?

11. Does the house have good bones? Quality workmanship?

12. Enough closet space and storage?

13. Two or more bathrooms? (Important for resale.)

14. Updated kitchen?

15. Enough room in the garage for the SUV?

16. Ask what kind of plumbing (copper pipes are best).

17. Date of last roof replacement/repairs?

18. Are the heating and air conditioning operational? Last repairs?

19. Have fireplaces and chimneys been maintained?

20. Ask to see where the property line begins and ends.

21. If there is a Homeowner's Association, find out the monthly dues and if there are any special assessments on the horizon.

It's always a good idea to keep a file of each property you visit and list the positives and negatives of each home. It will also keep you from visiting the same home twice.

GET PREPARED TO MAKE AN OFFER

Get a copy of a Residential Purchase Contract from your real estate agent, the local Multiple Listing Service or your local bar association and study it at your leisure in advance. This will prevent the jitters everyone experiences when it comes time to sign and you'll know exactly what you're signing.

It pays to do your homework in advance and to have your questions answered ahead of time. The measurable result? You will be operating in a mental state of confidence rather than fear.

PURCHASE PRICE –
10 TIPS ON HOW MUCH YOU SHOULD OFFER

We're getting close, and now it's finally time to make an offer. Here are some great tips I've compiled when it comes time to make an offer:

1. The selling price is set by the "law of supply and demand." Study the Comparable Properties, or "comps," with your agent.
   Make sure the comps are less than 6 months old (shorter time period in a rapidly changing market.)

2. All buyers should ask for and thoroughly read Seller Disclosures before writing an offer. This will inform you of any known defects about the property and will help you determine the appropriate price to offer.

3. Find out as much about the sellers as possible.
   (Within reason; you don't have to hire a private eye here!)
   The information you uncover will help you determine if there might be flexibility in the price.

4. Check the public records to see if their taxes are current and fully paid.
   Check to see how long they have lived on the property.

5. Get your agent to call the local title company and order a property profile to see what kind of shape their mortgage is in.
   Are they behind in their payments?

6. If the house has been on the market a while (more than 4 weeks), the buying public has voted that it isn't worth what the sellers are asking. In that case, don't offer full price.

7. If it has just come on the market and is exactly what you've been looking for, make the offer as close to asking price as possible.

8. The reaction to your offering price will be affected by the terms of your offer.

9. If you write a clean offer with no contingencies, the seller will most likely be flexible with the price.

10. If your offer has several inspection contingencies and/or if one home must be sold to buy another, the seller will most likely reject your offer.

A HOME WARRANTY IS CRUCIAL –
ASK THE SELLER TO PAY

Obtaining a Home Warranty on a home at the time of purchase is to the advantage of the buyer and the seller, but here's a little secret: The seller usually pays for the warranty. It protects the buyer from major expenses relating to appliances, plumbing, electrical problems, a/c and heating issues and a myriad of other unforeseen occurrences. It also limits the liability of the seller from having to pay for all of the repairs and a potential lawsuit.

Bottom line? The cost ranges from $250 to $500 for a one-year plan and the coverage lasts for one year. The buyer pays approximately $50 for each service call and the policy will cover the needed repairs.

YOUR OFFER IS ACCEPTED...
AND A LITTLE EARNEST MONEY, TOO!

A Purchase Offer must be accompanied by an *Earnest Money Deposit*, which typically amounts to 3% of the agreed upon purchase price. This proves to the seller that you are serious and are willing to put up cash to prove it. This deposit also serves as a source of damages if you walk away from the offer without a reason a month down the line. The earnest money counts toward the sum you'll need at closing.

ESCROW OPENS AND LET
THE INSPECTIONS ROLL

In your Purchase Offer you allowed for a minimum of a 7-day *Contingency Period* to perform all of your investigations. It is important to note that in most states you can walk away from the transaction without liabilities until your contingency period has expired. After that, your deposit is at risk. During the inspection period you can count on the fact that something unexpected will surface, but remember, **EVERYTHING** can be negotiated.

Here are the inspections that will generally occur:
- Termite Inspection.
- General Physical Inspection.
- Mold Inspection (if the general inspection sites danger zones).
- Appraisal of the property and possibly a land survey.
- Natural Hazard Inspection that will disclose if the property is in a flood zone, fire zone, earthquake fault zone, seismic hazard zone hurricane area or wild land area that may contain substantial forest fire risks and hazards.
- State government mandated retrofitting, which varies from city to city and includes inspections to see that low flow toilets are installed, water heaters are strapped, earthquake shut-off valves are in place and smoke detectors are functioning properly.
- Possible other inspections that might take place include asbestos and radon.
- Buyers might also ask for copies of utility bills to get a sense of the costs.

TIMBER!! LOOKOUT FOR THOSE TREES WITH DEEP, NASTY ROOTS

Trees are beautiful but their roots can play havoc when winding around sewage and drain lines or could pose a problem if a disease is present or they appear to be slanting.

Here is a solution:
- Call in an Arborist (see websites in back) to get a diagnosis to determine the tree's health and if the slanting poses a danger to the house or neighboring homes, then, negotiate the repairs with the seller.
- For tree root issues call your plumber or your local Roto Rooter to run a tiny video cam down through the drain pipes to make sure they are clear and damage free. Cost: $250.

HOW UNMARRIED COUPLES CAN BUY PROPERTY TOGETHER

First, ownership of real property can take many forms. These vary from state to state but some of the most common ways are the following:

SOLE OWNERSHIP. Ownership by a single person.

JOINT TENANCY. Probably the most common, this means two or more people have equal but undivided shares. This carries what's called "right of survivorship," which means if one owner dies, that person's shares automatically go over to the other owner or owners.

TENANCY BY THE ENTIRETIES. This is a variation on joint tenancy, in which the joint tenants are husband and wife, with each owning half and with neither permitted to sell the property without the agreement of the other.

TENANTS IN COMMON. Two or more people can hold title in this form in specific proportions spelled out in the title. If one owner dies, that person's share passes to the rightful heirs, not to the other owners, and those heirs become new tenants in common with the existing tenants in common.

COMMUNITY PROPERTY. This exists in a limited number of states as a variation on joint tenancy between husband and wife with each owning half. But in the event of death, the deceased's share passes in a manner similar to tenants in common, i.e., with no right of survivorship.

The best option for unmarried couples would be to consider taking title to the property as *Tenants in Common*.

That way you delineate exactly what share you own in the event you split up. However, there are other considerations that go along with this, so first discuss this with an attorney in the state you're buying the home. For example, your partner could sell his share to virtually anyone.

It's possible your attorney may also advise you on crafting a written agreement that defines financial responsibilities and how — in the event of a split — your household's assets will be divided, among other things, such as custody of pets.

Another option for unmarried couples is the increasingly popular Domestic-

Partner Agreement, where you also decide in advance who gets what, including property. This can also be used to spell out debt obligations; for example, who pays what household expenses, who uses what savings and checking accounts and who pays for insurance.

You can also agree in this document that you will go to arbitration, in the event a post-breakup dispute should arise. Realize that some state legal systems don't fully honor Domestic Partner Agreements, while others honor them only in select counties.

Nolo (www.nolo.com) which publishes do-it-yourself legal books, offers "Living Together: A Legal Guide for Unmarried Couples." Additionally, a website that explores legal options and documents for unmarried domestic partners is www.domparts.com

AND THE JOURNEY THROUGH ESCROW CONTINUES...

Here are some of the events that take place during the escrow process:

- A title insurance company conducts a title search to determine, among other things, whether the seller will be able to transfer a clean marketable title, free of liens and encumbrances to the buyer.
- The escrow company obtains demand statements from lenders and other creditors to be paid off before the escrow closes.
- The escrow company may obtain loan documents and instructions from the buyer's lender for the buyer to sign.
- The escrow company figures tax and interest pro-rations, prepares the closing paperwork and arranges for the buyers and sellers to sign the closing paperwork.
- Homeowner's Association documents are requested by the escrow company and reviewed and approved by the buyers.
- The buyers conduct a final "walk-through" of the property to confirm that the home is in the same condition as when the offer was accepted and

that any agreed-upon repairs have been completed satisfactorily. If the repairs have not been completed by the seller, the buyer should hire a contractor to provide a quote for unfinished repairs and submit a "Request for A Credit" from the seller and it must be approved by the seller before closing.

- After signatures are obtained from the buyers, the loan documents are sent back to the lender for funding.
- The escrow company records the necessary documents in the new buyer's names with the county where the property is located, thereby closing the transaction.
- The escrow company disburses the appropriate funds and sends copies of the closing paperwork to the appropriate parties.

Welcome home! The buyer can now pickup the keys and move in.

THE SECRETS OF BUYING A HOME

I hope you've found the home-buying tips up to this point particularly refreshing.

As a companion piece to such tips, I've also decided to let you in on a few closely-held industry secrets (one of my favorite parts):

LET THE SUNSHINE IN!
IF YOU DON'T, IT CAN COST YOU

When looking at properties to buy be sure to visit at different times during the day or study the sun exposure by evaluating the lot setting. Why bother? This can mean the difference between fading carpeting and drapes, more costly energy use, a swimming pool that sits in the shade most of the day, the need for solar screens and more sprinklers, to name just a few.

NOTE TO BUYERS: SELLER'S DON'T ALWAYS
TAKE THE HIGHEST OFFER

The contingency period, deposit amount, escrow period and terms can play a much bigger role in their decision.

Have your agent find out what terms are most important to the seller. If you can meet those terms, there is a very good chance they will be flexible with the price.

COMPELLING LETTERS TO THE SELLERS
REALLY DO WORK!

To make your offer stand out from the rest, write a heartfelt letter to the seller. It can be a simple introductory letter about you and your family and what features you like most about the house and why. You may also want to include a summary of your offer in this letter to make it easy and efficient for the seller to review. Include the following items but don't go overboard and do anything creepy like send along family and dog photos. This is simply to warm up your offer and put a face behind the numbers:

- Include your loan pre-approval letter from your lender.
- Your purchase price amount. If it's low, let them know it's because of needed repairs or that another house in the area recently sold for less.
- Your deposit amount and proposed escrow period.
- Give them the opportunity to select the title and escrow company.
- Offer them the opportunity to extend the escrow period if they need more time to move or allow them to lease the property back from you for a few months.

A SELLER'S DIVORCE OR DEATH DOESN'T EQUAL A DISCOUNT

Don't assume that if sellers are divorcing or are deceased that a low offer will be accepted due to the duress. Behind the scenes disagreements by participating family members may make it difficult to negotiate a low selling price, and your low ball offer may just backfire as a result of this bad timing.

ALWAYS INCLUDE AN EXPIRATION DATE ON YOUR OFFER

Be sure to write an expiration date on your offer to be 24 to 48 hours from the Purchase Offer date. This tactic is best used if negotiations are dragging on and will keep the seller in motion.

BE NICE...DON'T BURN ANY BRIDGES (IN THE BEGINNING)

Keep in mind that once your offer is accepted the negotiations have just begun. You will be working with the sellers for at least a month – or until the transaction closes. Negotiate as strongly as you feel necessary in the beginning, but remember that you may be looking for cooperation from your seller down the road and if you've burned bridges in the beginning you may not get the cooperation you are looking for. Be FIRM and FAIR.

SO YOU WANT TO CANCEL THE ESCROW... NOT SO FAST, ALL PARTIES MUST AGREE

Once the 7 to 14 day inspection period is over and all contingencies have been removed, if one party wants to cancel the escrow, the other party must agree, on paper, and release the deposit funds.

For this reason, it is wise to be calm, cordial and diplomatic when the decision is made to cancel the escrow. Disagreements should be handled through the agents. Remember, real estate agents cannot release deposit money without the written consent of both the buyer *and* seller.

IF THE SELLERS AREN'T OUT BY CLOSING, HAVE THEM SIGN A LEASEBACK AGREEMENT

Things happen and sometimes, even with the best laid plans the sellers can't be out by the closing date. If this should happen do not close the transaction until you have a signed *Leaseback Agreement* from the seller. Don't panic! Your agent will have the formal documents that need to be filled out, which state that both the buyer and seller are in agreement that the seller will lease the property back from the buyer for a fixed amount of time for an agreed upon price.

Additionally, any cancellation fees, utility costs or insurance coverage you incur due to the delay can be passed on to the seller. This will protect all parties involved and the transaction can still close on the scheduled date.

MOLD & MILDEW CAN GROW IN THE MOST UNUSUAL PLACES

Your general inspection does not include a thorough inspection for mold. The following is a list of areas where mold is commonly found:

Behind the refrigerator where the icemaker water line is connected. This is an often overlooked and an area where mold can grow rapidly when there is a tiny leak.

- In the attic or ceiling as a result of a leaky roof.
- Around windows where there might be a water leak.
- At the water connection behind the washer.
- Kitchen and bathroom sinks
- Around air conditioner if there is a wall unit.
- Under the patio door.

LIES ABOUT BUYING A HOME

Lies, lies and more lies. They're out there, making the world of real estate a dangerous one if you don't have a proper guide. In addition to your own personal real estate agent, I hope this little "tell-all" section of the book helps prepare you to walk through your next Open House with eyes wide open:

PETS ARE NOT ALLOWED HERE!
(MAYBE & MAYBE NOT)

In many states, such as California, there is now a Pet Discrimination Law that prohibits Homeowner's Associations from enforcing a "No Pets Allowed" policy.

One call to your governor's office will tell you if and when the bill was passed in your state. Most of the Homeowner's Associations aren't aware of this law and will put up a fight. Do your homework and make that call. I have fought and won this battle for clients on many occasions.

IF THE SELLER DIES, THE TRANSACTION DIES

Not true. The seller signed a legal and binding contact. Therefore, their estate is obligated to complete the transaction. Anticipate a delay while the paperwork is being processed. In most states, if the buyer dies during the escrow process, their estate is no longer required to complete the transaction. This information is outlined in your Purchase Contract.

BEING PRE-QUALIFIED FOR A LOAN AND
PRE-APPROVED FOR A LOAN ARE REALLY
THE SAME THING

Wrong.

Becoming Pre-Qualified for a loan consists of a 5-minute conversation with a mortgage broker you've never met or spoken to before.

He/she will ask you a series of questions about your employment, income, debt and funds for a down payment. This information will not be verified but 99% of the time they will immediately fax you over a "Pre-Qualification" letter for a loan.

At this point, the lender is under no obligation or commitment to give you a loan. Bottom line: These Pre-Qualification letters are not worth the paper they are written on and are quite unimpressive to any seller. Loan pre-approval is the path to take and here is how you get there:

- Contact your lender and let them know you want to be pre-approved for a mortgage loan.
- You will fill out a lengthy application and provide tax returns, pay stubs and bank statements.
- All of the information will be verified by the lender and your credit will be examined.
- A formal "Letter of Approval" will be drafted by a Loan Officer.

IT'S ALWAYS BETTER TO BUY THAN TO RENT

Not necessarily. Although buyers boast about the advantages of permanency and ownership, diehard renters enjoy the freedom their lifestyles provide. From hassle-free maintenance to the record number of luxury amenities present in new properties, many renters are perfectly content to stay that way.

Here are some pros and cons to consider when determining whether to buy or rent:

RENTERS

- The only upfront cost is the first and last month's rent.
- Don't gain or lose equity.
- Realize no property related tax advantages.
- Enjoy the assurance of fixed costs that won't fluctuate during the term of a lease.
- Can pack up and leave upon the expiration of their leases. They don't

face the hassle of finding a buyer and waiting until a sale takes place.
- Often enjoy the convenience of a full-time maintenance staff to handle lawn maintenance, appliance and other repairs.

BUYERS

- Must put down a substantial down payment.
- Often gain equity.
  However, they can also lose it.
- Must go through the process of selling their homes and finding a buyer.
- Pay high homeowner's insurance premiums.
- Are subject to variable costs in the absence of documentation that keeps costs fixed (such as a lease agreement).
- Must either perform maintenance/repairs on their own or using the services of a professional whom they hire and pay themselves.

In some gated communities, the residents pay a maintenance fee for the convenience of having yard work and general maintenance performed by a full-time staff.

- Are free to paint, redecorate and remodel their homes as often as they wish (unless the property is governed by a Homeowner's Association.)
- Benefit from tax advantages associated with homeownership.
- Eventually own their homes and are free of a monthly mortgage payment.
- Owning a home is a big part of the American Dream and can provide sub stantial financial and psychological rewards. However, if you plan to stay in a home for less than 5-7 years, the costs associated with buying and selling a home might not only eat up any profits gained by appreciation, but may even cause you to lose money.

ALL COSTS RELATED TO OWNING A HOME ARE TAX DEDUCTIBLE

Some buyers think, hope, they can write off everything connected with the house. Not so. Here is a list of fees that are NOT tax deductible:

- Homeowner's Association fees
- Property insurance
- Private mortgage insurance
- Basic maintenance and repairs
- Even though these fees are not tax deductible, if you convert the home to rental property or sell it, these costs will affect the property's tax basis.

PART 3
MORTGAGES
& CREDIT
TIPS, SECRETS & LIES
YOU NEED TO KNOW

TIPS ON MORTGAGES

If its one single complaint my clients have about buying or selling a new home, it would have to be the sore subject of mortgages.

Buyers complain about the fairly invasive nature of obtaining a loan and sellers endure no shortage of heartaches when deals close to closing fall through because the buyer couldn't swing the loan.

To try and take some of the headache out of this process, I've compiled my usual battery of tips, secrets and lies to make it a tad less painful.

TYPES OF MORTGAGES TO LOOK FOR

Unless you have enough money to pay for a house with cash, you'll need a mortgage. A mortgage is a loan to finance the purchase of a home and is a promise to make regular payments until the loan is paid off.

There are so many different types of loans out there it's mind-numbing. What you need to know is that most of them are variations of a fixed-rate mortgage or an adjustable rate mortgage. You might also want to know about a reverse mortgage. Having knowledge of these basic loan programs will help you understand how they all work:

FIXED-RATE MORTGAGES have a fixed interest rate over the entire term of the loan <u>that never changes</u>. If you are interested in a consistent payment/no surprises loan, this is probably the best alternative.

The typical terms for these loans are 15 or 30 years. Now there are even 40 year mortgages available.

ADJUSTABLE RATE MORTGAGES (ARMS) are loans that are fixed for an introductory period, after which the rate adjusts to a new level based upon a pre-determined financial market index. Traditionally, the ARMs offer consumers lower initial rates to keep the monthly mortgage payments low. The typical initial term for ARMs is between 1 and 7 years – the longer the initial term, the higher the starting rate.

After the fixed-rate period expires, if the interest rates are more attractive, you can refinance to another short term or fixed-rate program.

A REVERSE MORTGAGE can be obtained by homeowners who are at least 62 years old. This is a mortgage where a homeowner can tap into a portion of their home's equity without selling their house or taking out a home-equity loan. Unlike a traditional mortgage requiring monthly principal and interest payments, a reverse mortgage-lender pays the homeowner instead. Your equity decreases as your mortgage balance increases each month, yet you will never owe more than the value of your home – even if the value of the mortgage ultimately exceeds that. For people who are house rich and cash poor, a reverse mortgage can be a real saving situation. For more information visit **www.rmaarp.com.**

MORTGAGE BANKERS, MORTGAGE BROKERS, CREDIT UNIONS, APPRAISERS & UNDERWRITERS: *WHO THESE PEOPLE ARE AND WHAT YOU NEED TO KNOW*

Who are all these men and women in suits asking you questions and standing in the way of buying or selling your home? Here is a quick "scorecard" of the major players and what they do:

MORTGAGE BANKERS are in business to make mortgage loans, handle the monthly paperwork and service the loans. They either retain their loans in a portfolio or sell them off to investors. The upside is that they work with their own money and can make underwriting decisions more quickly. The only downside is that their rates may not be competitive and/or they may have limited loan products available to the market.

MORTGAGE BROKERS make no loans at all and do not service loans. They bring borrowers and lenders together like "matchmakers." The upside to working with mortgage brokers is that they work with multiple lenders, which allows them a large menu of loan products to offer their clients. The downside is that they do not control the loan approval process.

CREDIT UNIONS exist to provide financial assistance to their members.

While they are doing more home loans these days and may not be competitive with the commercial lenders nor have as many loan products, their lender fees are often less than traditional lenders.

THE APPRAISER is a person who is licensed by the state and hired by your lender to estimate the value of the property you are buying.

UNDERWRITING is the lender's process of analyzing your mortgage application and making a decision about furnishing the loan. You will be judged on two basic criteria: Your ability to meet your obligations in the future and your willingness to do so. To be on the lookout for indicators of both, your employment and credit history will be carefully scrutinized during this process.

CHECK YOUR OWN CREDIT BEFORE MEETING THE LENDER

Preparation is key when trying to make the mortgage process as stress-free as possible. Here are three companies who will provide you with the information you'll need, quickly and accurately, before meeting with your lender of choice:

Experian 1-888-397-3742   http://www.experian.com

Equifax 1-800-685-1111 http://www.equifax.com

TransUnion 1-800-916-8800 http://www.transunion.com

SECRETS ABOUT MORTGAGES & CREDIT

YOUR CREDIT CARD COMPANIES ARE WATCHING YOU

Many borrowers are surprised to learn about the *Universal Default Clause*, small-print item you probably agreed to when applying for your most recent credit card. The *Universal Default Clause* allows credit card companies to charge you a 29.9 percent interest rate (or higher) if you ever make a late payment on any one credit card, even if that card isn't issued by the company charging the higher interest rate. Credit card companies periodically pull your credit report and raise your interest rate based on the history of other accounts you maintain. Credit card companies say that they believe your behavior on one credit card might be the same on all credit cards.

VENDORS WHO HAVE SUBMITTED INACCURATE INFORMATION TO THE CREDIT REPORTING AGENCY MUST RESPOND WITHIN 30 DAYS

A credit report is not always as fault-free as we might hope.

Here are some developments that can trip you up if you're not careful:

- Vendors cannot submit negative information about you to the credit bureau and then disappear. They must be reachable and respond to your inquiry within 30 days.
- Credit reporting agencies will temporarily remove negative items while you are attempting to resolve outstanding issues but will they will not be removed permanently until the vendor submits a release.

CREDIT MISTAKES THAT LOWER FICO SCORES:

Credit report not what you thought it might be? Here are some possible ways you might have stumbled in the past:

- Late Payments
- Unpaid Accounts
- Excessive credit inquiries
- Too many credit cards
- Maximum credit limits used
- Bankruptcies, judgments, foreclosures, liens

HOW DOES YOUR CREDIT SCORE RANK?

Interpretations of credit scores vary from lender to lender but the following is a guideline:

SCORE	RATING:
800-850	Excellent
700-800	Great
650-700	Good
600-650	Fair
400-600	Marginal
Under 400	Not so good

7 WAYS TO IMPROVE YOUR CREDIT SCORE BEFORE APPLYING FOR A HOME LOAN

What can you do to help your odds during the approval process? A mortgage lender can expedite credit report corrections faster than the consumer because they deal directly with the sales reps at the credit bureaus. However, there are a variety of ways you can improve your credit score before applying for that loan:

PAY YOUR BILLS ON TIME. Recent late payments are more harmful to your credit score than older late payments. Starting today will make a bigger difference than you might think.

PAY YOUR LARGEST BILLS FIRST. The larger the missed payment the more damage it does to your credit rating.

PAY DOWN YOUR CREDIT CARDS. Your account balances should be 50 percent of your available credit.

DON'T HAVE TOO MANY OPEN LINES OF CREDIT. Unused credit is a potential red flag to lenders because you can rack up instant debt when you are pre-approved for a loan.

SCALE DOWN. Hold off on any large purchases until you have closed escrow on your new home. Many lenders pull a second credit report just prior to closing.

CONSOLIDATE DEBT ONTO TWO OR THREE CREDIT CARDS. Remember, if you are consolidating your credit card balances try not to exceed 50 percent of that card's credit limit.

 DO NOT CANCEL OLD CREDIT CARDS. Canceling old credit cards can actually lower your credit score by making your credit history appear shorter. Newer accounts should be closed first.

YOUR CREDIT SCORE IS MORE IMPORTANT THAN YOUR SALARY

If your credit score is high enough some lenders won't consider your salary before giving you the lowest available interest rate. Indeed, your credit score is perhaps the most important factor in determining whether lenders approve your mortgage loan or car loan. It matters more than your annual salary and much more than your net worth.

3 MAJOR CREDIT BUREAUS HAVE GOT YOUR NUMBER

Before assigning one score, most lenders consider your scores from the three major credit bureaus (TransUnion, Equifax and Experian). The lenders will assign the middle score to you when determining your interest rate for any given loan. For instance, if Experian gives you a 721 credit rating, TransUnion gives you a 719, and Equifax a 601, lenders will consider 719 to be your credit score. Because of this, you should monitor your report from each of the 3 bureaus.

THOSE 3 LITTLE NUMBERS CAN
HAVE A 6 DIGIT IMPACT

Those who have lower credit scores must tolerate high interest rates on their credit cards, mortgages and car loans. Keep in mind that a low score can also mean an increase in your automobile insurance premiums. Yes… insurance companies are also watching. Keep in mind that anyone who may have an interest in you professionally or even romantically can easily check your credit rating.

MAKING A LATE PAYMENT IS THE
BIGGEST OFFENSE

Your payment history accounts for about 35 percent of your credit score. Late payments within six months have the greatest impact on your score while late payments more than 24 months old have little impact on your score. The credit scoring models assume that your current behavior is a far more important indicator of your credit worthiness than your past behavior.

GIVE YOUR CHILDREN A BOOST

Consider adding your high school and college-aged children to your credit card accounts. If you have good credit and you add your children as authorized users to your credit card accounts, you will help them build their credit scores so that they enter adulthood with strong credit. If you feel uncomfortable handing over the credit card you can simply add his or her name to your account.

POTENTIAL EMPLOYERS CAN
TAKE A DEEPER LOOK

Increasing your credit score can make you more employable. Some companies consider your credit score to be more than your financial reputation. In fact, employers consider it to be a sign of your character. Some companies, especially those hiring employees who handle money, will not hire a person with poor credit.

KEEPING CREDIT CARD ACCOUNTS
OPEN IS A GOOD THING

Closing your credit card accounts can hurt your credit score. The length of time you have credit can affect your credit score by 15 percent. Closing a credit card account or not using it will lower the average age of your accounts and possibly lower your total credit rating.

CONSUMER CREDIT COUNSELING?
PROCEED WITH CAUTION

Consumer Credit Counseling will not directly hurt your credit score but here are some things to consider: A consumer credit counseling company will handle all matters regarding your debt. Creditors will not call you when a bill is late, they will call the consumer credit counseling company. If the company fails to pay your bill on time, you will not know because the creditor has stopped communicating with you. The only way to guard against this is to thoroughly investigate consumer reports on the credit counseling company before hiring them.

LIES ABOUT MORTGAGES

There are a lot of myths, theories, urban legends and outright lies about the mortgage approval process. Here I will try to debunk the worst of them:

HAD A BANKRUPTCY?
FORGET ABOUT GETTING A MORTGAGE

False. While declaring bankruptcy can be serious business, it's not the deal breaker many assume it to be. If you have had to declare bankruptcy in the past, here are two reasons why you shouldn't count yourself out of the race before even lining up at the gate:

NOTHING IS "FOREVER." A bankruptcy legally can remain on your credit report for up to 10 years, but its effect on your credit score can start to diminish the day your case is closed. Adopt responsible credit habits such as paying your bills on time, using only a small portion of your available credit and not applying for too much credit at once are the fastest ways get your credit back on track.

NOT ALL LOANS ARE CREATED EQUALLY. It can actually be easier to get a mortgage after a bankruptcy than to get other types of installment loans. You may be able to qualify for a high-rate mortgage as little as six months after a bankruptcy and a very competitive rate 1 to 2 years after a bankruptcy. Do your homework. There are many mortgage bankers who specialize in mortgages after bankruptcy.

IF LENDERS DON'T ASK ABOUT
A PAST FORECLOSURE;
DON'T TELL

False. Every mortgage loan application asks if you have ever had a foreclosure. If you fudge on the application, the foreclosure will most likely show up on a credit report. Even if it doesn't show up and you do get the loan, if the lender finds out that you lied on your application you could be sued and/or fined very serious penalties.

SEVERAL MISSED
MORTGAGE PAYMENTS.
NEXT STEP,
FORECLOSURE

- Not necessarily. If you are even several months behind many lenders will try to help you in the following ways:
- Restructure your loan allowing you to make lower payments.
- Forgo interest for a period of time.

LENDERS ARE ON YOUR SIDE

False. There are "predatory lenders" who take advantage of unsuspecting borrowers in the following ways:
- Misrepresent a borrower's credit score to place them in a mortgage interest rate category that is higher than their credit score indicates. In this case, lenders prey upon the elderly and those who are not proficient in English.
- The lender may offer a low interest rate but the discount points and other fees will be very high.
- Lenders may charge unnecessary "junk" fees such as administrative, processing, origination and documentation fees to name a few. These are pure lender profits and can be negotiated.
- Some lenders quote abnormally low closing fees and then impose higher costs at the closing leaving the borrower little choice but to pay or walk away and lose the property.

TO PAY YOUR MONTHLY
BALANCE OR NOT TO PAY

Most people believe that they must keep a balance on their credit card to keep a good credit score. This causes many consumers to make unnecessary interest payments. The truth is that credit bureaus have no way of knowing whether you pay your balance in full or make monthly payments. If you have the financial resources to do so, pay off your balance each month. It can't hurt your credit score; in fact, it might help your score by lowering your utilization rate (which is the debt you carry in proportion to your limit.)

PART 4
STAYING OUT
OF COURT
TIPS YOU NEED TO KNOW ABOUT REDUCING YOUR RISK AND STAYING OUT OF COURT IN A REAL ESTATE TRANSACTION

TIPS ON STAYING OUT OF COURT

There is nothing worse than tainting the success of buying or selling a home with the grim specter of unpleasant – and unnecessary – litigation. Since "*Secrets* and *Lies*" are what generally land people in court, this section will focus on "*Tips*" that will help reduce your risk of being sued during the home buying and selling process.

GOOD INSPECTIONS ARE YOUR BEST DEFENSE

Much like in football, the best defense starts with a good offense. In other words, the more you do to avoid legal ramifications *now* the more likely you are to stay out of court *later*.

Case in point: the most significant events that occur during the home buying and selling process are the inspections. It is at this stage where many real estate transactions are renegotiated or cancelled. **WARNING:** _Bad inspections are the basis on which most lawsuits are created_. Buyers want the home inspections to uncover any hidden problems and sellers want them to show they have made a serious effort to discover and disclose any issues that might exist in the home that they might not be aware of.

Performing your own due diligence and hiring qualified inspectors are the two most important factors during the inspection process and will significantly reduce your risk of being involved in a lawsuit.

But where to begin? The answer is right here!

THE TOP 5 QUALIFICATIONS A HOME INSPECTOR MUST HAVE:

1) Must be a licensed general contractor.
2) Must carry and provide a copy of current Errors and Omissions and Liability Insurance.

3) Must be bonded.

4) Must be a member of professional trade organizations that require a Standard Code of Ethics and provide ongoing training. They should be a member of your state inspection association as well as the following two national associations:

- American Society of Home Inspectors (ASHI)
- National Assn. of Home Inspectors (NAHI)
- Three to five years of experience working in your area.
  (Make sure to ask them if they have any lawsuits pending.)

PERFORM YOUR OWN INSPECTIONS, TOO. DON'T JUST RELY ON THE PROFESSIONALS

As with any other major transaction in your life, there is no substitute for personal accountability. Even though you will hire a qualified inspector, I strongly recommend performing your own visual inspection, not as an "either/or" but as an "also/and."

The following are comprehensive "Visual Inspection Checklists" (to check both inside and outside the home) used by most real estate brokers and agents. These checklists are intended to help you conduct a reasonably competent and diligent visual inspection of the accessible areas of the property.

INTERIOR VISUAL INSPECTION CHECKLIST

CEILINGS – check for stains, sagging or cracks.

WALLS – check for cracks, stains or holes.

WINDOWS – water or mildew stains, fogged or broken panes, cracks around frames.

DOORS – uneven spaces between door and jamb, cracks around frames.

FLOORS – sloping, cracked or missing tiles, defects in the floor or floor covering. Always look underneath rugs.

STAIRS/STEPS/RAILINGS – broken, uneven loose steps or damaged railing.

FIREPLACE – cracks, separated from wall, broken hearth.

KITCHEN & BATHROOMS – grout or tiles missing, stains, cracks.

PLUMBING – visible signs of leaking above or below the sinks, faucets, pipes, toilet tank, showers/bathtubs.

WATER HEATER – earthquake straps, visible signs of leaking.

ELECTRICAL – broken light fixtures, exposed wiring, burned or missing outlet covers, check to see if outlets are grounded.

STRUCTURE – signs of room addition or modifications.

BASEMENT – cracks, white powdery deposits on walls, sump/ejector pump.

EXTERIOR VISUAL INSPECTION CHECKLIST

ROOF – missing, cracked or damaged shingles or tiles.

SIDEWALKS/DRIVEWAYS – cracks, uneven, tilted.

STEPS/STAIRS – broken, uneven, loose steps or missing railings.

DECKS/PATIOS – cracked slabs, sloping toward house, pulling away from house. Patio should sit above the ground. A sunken patio will collect water and create a flood hazard.

STRUCTURE – signs of room addition or modifications.

FOUNDATION/SLAB – cracks.

CHIMNEY – cracks, separation from wall.

STUCCO OR SIDING – cracks, patches or seams

LANDSCAPING – soil erosion, drainage, hillside instability, bowed or cracked retaining walls, leaning or rotted fences, leaning trees, cracked sidewalks around trees.

DOORS/WINDOWS – distorted frames, cracked glass, moisture stains around windows indicating possible leakage and mold.

SWIMMING POOL/SPA – cracks, missing tiles, loose or separated coping/decking, excess moisture in the ground around pool could indicate possible leak in pool.

GARAGE – stains, floor slab cracked or separated from adjacent foundation.

GUTTERS – check to see if they are visible and in tact

MATERIAL FACTS AND FULL DISCLOSURE

As previously mentioned in this book, any fact that could affect a buyer's decision to buy a property absolutely *must* be disclosed.

In the area of disclosure, you must let your conscience be your guide. You know the positive features of your home by heart. Likewise, you know the sticking points that sometimes keep you up at night. They are what need to be disclosed. Here are some examples of overlooked disclosures that have landed sellers in court:

- Failing to disclose a death or suicide on a property that occurred within the past three years.
- Failing to disclose that foghorns go off in the wintertime in the middle of the night.
- Failing to disclose that at certain times of the year farmers are allowed to plow all night for several months.
- Failing to disclose that freight trains can be clearly heard blowing their horns 3 times per week.
- Failing to disclose that the housing development was built next to or on top of a former waste (or even worse, toxic waste) dump or cemetery.
- Failing to disclose that a metro-line, fire station or airport are in close proximity and can be clearly heard.
- Failing to disclose that a halfway house or registered sex offender is in close proximity.

PERMITS, PERMITS...WHO NEEDS PERMITS?

You do! If you are planning improvements or remodeling projects on your property, you must first obtain a permit from your local Department of Building and Safety. This is no mere luxury; if you want to keep things above board, it's a necessity.

Why? The reason is quite simple: If you do not obtain necessary building and mechanical permits, you will receive a hefty fine by the city.

This can be a shock for those who are new to the do-it-yourself renovation arena. However, it's serious business to local inspectors and skipping this relatively simple step can cost you thousands of dollars in the long run. Additionally, the appraisal on your property will not include the square footage in those new rooms or new additions *without a permit*.

It's much easier to simply go by the book in the short run. The cost is approximately $20 to $40 for each permit and in most cities you can apply for the permits online. The following improvements and/or remodeling jobs require a permit in most every state:

- Roof replacement
- New Heating/Air Conditioning system
- Electrical system replacement
- New pool
- Removing a pool and filling in with dirt
- Replacing windows
- Kitchen remodel
- Bathroom remodel
- New room addition of any kind
- New cement patio (because it can change grading)
- Converted garage
- New drains and pipes
- Water heater or furnace replacement
- New plumbing

WHEN IS A HANDYMAN NOT A HANDYMAN?

There comes a time when do-it-yourself just can't be done on your lonesome. In such cases, there are plenty of willing and capable industry professionals to service a variety of home improvement needs. But that begs the question: When will a simple handyman suffice and when do you need to call in the big guns?

In most states, a handyman can perform household services that do not exceed $500 per project.

Any projects that exceed $500 should be performed by a licensed contractor. To be sure, visit local, county or state websites to learn this valuable information.

OPEN HOUSES AND INSURANCE COVERAGE

Think holding an Open House is as easy as blowing up a few balloons and planting a sign in the front yard? Think again. Before you or your agent holds an Open House check to be sure that you have the appropriate homeowner's insurance coverage to cover anyone who may take a tumble down the stairs or trip and break something on your property.

Here is a list of things you can do to minimize your risk of being sued if you do not have the appropriate insurance policy in place:

Apply red tape to any "danger zone" areas such as a low hanging tree branch, cracked stairs, cracks in the floor, unstable ceilings or any other areas where a guest might be at risk.

- Post signs where the ground slopes or the soil is soft.
- Post signs if there are animals on the property.
- Include a waiver on the "Open House Sign-In Sheet" that excludes the seller of any liability. Make sure everyone signs in as they walk in the door.

CHECK THE CHIMNEY...
IF NOT, IT CAN COST YOU THOUSANDS

Unless Santa is your inspector, the chimney is often overlooked in a real estate transaction. Buyers think that the general inspectors will inspect it and the sellers are unaware there is a problem. The truth is that your general inspector will check to see if it is operational and that is about as far as they go with their inspection.

There are many different components that need to be checked by a professional chimney inspector. They do this by running a video camera down the interior and performing a thorough evaluation of all of the components. In many older homes, the chimneys can be cracked exposing homeowners to potentially hazardous gases.

To replace a chimney flue the cost is a modest $120. However, in many cases, especially in older homes, the chimneys can be cracked and the cost to repair will run around $15,000.

TO ERR IS HUMAN... ESPECIALLY WHEN IT'S ON THE SIDE OF CAUTION

I could go on and on with the horror stories I've heard – and seen firsthand – about real estate induced litigation over the years, but my intention here is not to depress you or fill the sale or purchase of your home with doom and gloom.

However, I feel duty-bound to warn you of simple, cost-effective and necessary ways to reduce your chance of legal problems when it comes to buying or selling a home.

The fact is that we live in a litigious society. Whether you realize it or not, there are people who go to Open Houses simply to see if there is an opportunity to exploit your inexperience or naiveté. There are predators that make a living off of baiting you into not disclosing various issues about your home, only to turn around months after purchase and threaten to sue.

Don't let them. Arm yourself with preparation, knowledge and, most of all, caution. I said it when we started this journey together and I'll remind you of it here, as we end our time together: buying or selling a home has never been easier; it's also never been harder.

It's not like the old days when you put up a "for sale" sign and welcomed all comers with milk and cookies. Nowadays too many people are lactose intolerant or allergic to the peanuts in your homemade cookies!

It is important to err on the side of caution in such matters. Like we say in Beverly Hills, you can never be too thin, too rich, or too careful!

PART 5
PUTTING IT ALL TOGETHER
YOU'VE FINISHED THE BOOK!
NOW WHAT?
PUTTING IT ALL TOGETHER,
OF COURSE!

Congratulations! You have just made it through a "crash course" on *Secrets, Tips, and Lies When Buying or Selling a Home*. No easy feat at that! Particularly when I realize you didn't read this book in a vacuum. No doubt there were real-life pit stops, follies, frustrations and achievements in your own quest to buy or sell your home along the way. So you are to be doubly congratulated!

I am glad that we shared this time together. My goal was to provide current and cutting-edge information gathered from my own experiences as well as from my colleagues, many of whom rank in the top 100 real estate professionals in the world.

By now I trust you are better informed than when you started. Whether you are buying your first home or selling your twenty-first, there is power in knowledge. The journey does not begin – or end – with this book. I challenge you to keep reading, keep learning, keep investigating, and keep gaining that all-powerful knowledge that will arm you in this real estate battle.

For starters, you can visit my website, **www.KarenNorrisEstates.com**, where there is a host of free resources to compliment the information you've found here. Subscribe to my monthly newsletter and actually read it. Consider it a "live update" to this book every time you get an email from me. I strive to provide up-to-the-minute information from a variety of sources, and always include a personally-written article that expands on, and even adds to, what I've provided for you here. Sign up for my newsletter by sending an email to me at **KarenSNorris@yahoo.com**.

As always, I am free to answer questions and truly value your comments, suggestions and recommendations. You can send an email with any questions you might have to **KarenSNorris@yahoo.com**. I look forward to hearing from you. My favorite emails and letters are those that document real estate success stories; may yours be my next!

Remember, you are not alone! You have a wealth of information at your fingertips… use it! Take responsibility for your own actions but also demand professionalism and courtesy from your agent should you decide to work with one.

In any event, I wish you the best on your real estate journey. It is a challenging trip, full of ups and downs and bends in the road, but my hope is that when you reach your final destination you are satisfied not just with the endgame, but also many steps you took along the way.

NOTES

APPENDIX:
REAL ESTATE TERMS, RESOURCES & RECOMMENDATIONS

YOUR 3-PART HARMONY OF ORGANIZATIONS & WEBSITES, BOOKS AND REAL ESTATE TERMS

Secrets, Tips and Lies are only the beginning of your knowledge base. Along the way I've pointed to various websites, books and other resources I find most helpful in my own practice, and recommend liberally to my clients, colleagues and, yes, even competitors! In this final section I've gathered them all – websites, books and list of Real Estate Terms – to arm you with all you'll need to forge ahead in your quest to either buy or sell a home.

I've talked at length about the importance of staying up-to-date and current. Nowhere is it easier to do that than on the internet. Here I've gathered websites ranging from house hunting to mortgage and financial information. Check these out, bookmark the ones you like, and feel free to explore their various links and referral pages to find new favorites of your own. When you do, please don't hesitate to let me know about them!

I've collected my four favorite titles. Again, they are just the beginning; feel free to explore your favorite resources for more and, again, don't forget to let me in on the news when you do find a title to add.

HELPFUL WEBSITES FOR HOMEBUYERS & SELLERS

HOUSE HUNTING (NEW AND RESALE)

Realtor.com
Homestore.com
HomeSeekers.com
Cyberhomes.com

NEW HOME SITES

HomeBuilders.com

NewHomeNetwork.com

NewHomes.com

BuilderOnline.com

MHousing.com

Manufacturedhousing.com

SELLERS/FOR SALE BY OWNER

HouseValues.com

ForSaleByOwner.com

Owners.com

Americas-real-estate.com

Ebay.com

REAL ESTATE NEWS & ADVICE SITES

RealtyTimes.com

Inman.com

RealtorMag.com

Realtor.org

IRED.com

EXCELLENT SITE FOR RANKING AND INVESTIGATING SCHOOLS

Schoolmatters.com

GreatSchools.net

COMPREHENSIVE INFORMATION ON SCHOOL TEACHERS NATIONWIDE

www.nctq.org/cb

MORTGAGE & FINANCIAL INFORMATION

Mortgage.com

Interest.com

Eloan.com

Mortgage Bankers Association – MBAA.

GREAT VENDOR SITES

ANGIESLIST.COM – A word-of-mouth network for consumers. It has 425,000 subscribers, who generally pay $530 for access to anonymous reports on thousands of companies and contractors. Contractors do not pay to be on the list. Types of vendors include contractors, builders, handymen, housekeepers, landscapers, plumbers, electricians and just about every other service you can think of.

SERVICEMAGIC.COM – Contractors, not consumers, pay to join this service which includes anonymous customer ratings. Offers a "service guarantee" of up to $500 for dissatisfied customers but says most disputes are resolved when it acts as a mediator.

GETVENDORS.COM – This free site matches consumers with pros.

HELPFUL ORGANIZATIONS TO KNOW ABOUT

National Association of Realtors **www.realtor.com**
American Society of Home Inspectors **www.ashi.org**

National Association of Home Inspectors **www.nahi.org**
Environmental Protection Agency **(lead paint) www.epa.gov/lead**
Environmental Protection Agency **(asbestos) www.epa.gov/asbestos**
American Industrial Hygienists Association **(mold) www.aiha.org**
American Indoor Air Quality Council **(mold) www.aiaqc.org**
American Conference of Governmental Industrial Hygienists **(mold) www.acgih.org**
Megan's Law **www.registeredoffenderlist.org**
A National Database of Sex Offenders & Criminals **www.watchdog.us**
Department of Housing and Urban Development (Federal Fair Housing)
www.hud.gov/offices/theo

REAL ESTATE TERMS YOU NEED TO KNOW

A

AMENITY: a feature of the home or property that serves as a benefit to the buyer but that is not necessary to its use; may be natural (like location, woods, water) or man-made (like a swimming pool or garden).

AMORTIZATION: repayment of a mortgage loan through monthly install-ments of principal and interest; the monthly payment amount is based on a schedule that will allow you to own your home at the end of a specific time peri-od (for example, 15 or 30 years).

ANNUAL PERCENTAGE RATE (APR): calculated by using a standard formula, the APR shows the cost of a loan; expressed as a yearly inter-est rate, it includes the interest, points, mortgage insurance, and other fees associated with the loan.

APPLICATION: the first step in the official loan approval process; this form is used to record important information about the potential borrower nec-essary to the underwriting process.

APPRAISAL: a document that gives an estimate of a property's fair market value; an appraisal is generally required by a lender before loan approval to ensure that the mortgage loan amount is not more than the value of the property.

APPRAISER: a qualified individual who uses his or her experience and knowledge to prepare the appraisal estimate.

ARM: Adjustable Rate Mortgage; a mortgage loan subject to changes in inter-est rates; when rates change, ARM monthly payments increase or decrease at intervals determined by the lender; the change in monthly -payment amount, how-ever, is usually subject to a cap.

ASSESSOR: a government official who is responsible for determining the value of a property for the purpose of taxation.

ASSUMABLE MORTGAGE: a mortgage that can be transferred from a seller to a buyer; once the loan is assumed by the buyer the seller is no longer responsible for repaying it; there may be a fee and/or a credit package involved in the transfer of an assumable mortgage.

B

BALLOON MORTGAGE: a mortgage that typically offers low rates for an initial period of time (usually 5, 7, or 10) years; after that time period elapses, the balance is due or is refinanced by the borrower.

BANKRUPTCY: a federal law whereby a person's assets are turned over to a trustee and used to pay off outstanding debts; this usually occurs when someone owes more than they have the ability to repay.

BORROWER: a person who has been approved to receive a loan and is then obligated to repay it and any additional fees according to the loan terms.

BUILDING CODE: based on agreed upon safety standards within a specific area, a building code is a regulation that determines the design, construction, and materials used in building.

BUDGET: a detailed record of all income earned and spent during a specific period of time.

C

CAP: a limit, such as that placed on an adjustable rate mortgage, on how much a monthly payment or interest rate can increase or decrease.

CASH RESERVES: a cash amount sometimes required to be held in reserve in addition to the down payment and closing costs; the amount is determined by the lender.

CERTIFICATE OF TITLE: a document provided by a qualified source (such as a title company) that shows the property legally belongs to the current owner; before the title is transferred at closing, it should be clear <u>and</u> free of all liens or other claims.

CLOSING: also known as settlement, this is the time at which the property is formally sold and transferred from the seller to the buyer; it is at this time that the borrower takes on the loan obligation, pays all closing costs, and receives title from the seller.

CLOSING COSTS: customary costs above and beyond the sale price of the property that must be paid to cover the transfer of ownership at closing; these costs generally vary by geographic location and are typically detailed to the borrower after submission of a loan application.

COMMISSION: an amount, usually a percentage of the property sales price, which is collected by a real estate professional as a fee for negotiating the transaction.

CONDOMINIUM: a form of ownership in which individuals purchase and own a unit of housing in a multi-unit complex; the owner also shares financial responsibility for common areas.

CONVENTIONAL LOAN: a private sector loan, one that is not guaranteed or insured by the U.S. government.

COOPERATIVE (CO-OP): residents purchase stock in a cooperative corporation that owns a structure; each stockholder is then entitled to live in a specific unit of the structure and is responsible for paying a portion of the loan.

CREDIT HISTORY: history of an individual's debt payment; lenders use this information to gauge a potential borrower's ability to repay a loan.

CREDIT REPORT: a record that lists all past and present debts and the timeliness of their repayment; it documents an individual's credit history.

CREDIT BUREAU SCORE: a number representing the possibility a borrower may default; it is based upon credit history and is used to determine ability to qualify for a mortgage loan.

D

DEBT-TO-INCOME RATIO: a comparison of gross income to housing and non-housing expenses. With the FHA, the-monthly mortgage payment should be no more than 29% of monthly gross income (before taxes) and the mortgage payment combined with non-housing debts should not exceed 41% of income.

DEED: the document that transfers ownership of a property.

DEED-IN-LIEU: to avoid foreclosure ("in lieu" of foreclosure), a deed is given to the lender to fulfill the obligation to repay the debt; this process doesn't allow the borrower to remain in the house but helps avoid the costs, time, and effort associated with foreclosure.

DEFAULT: the inability to pay monthly mortgage payments in a timely manner or to otherwise meet the mortgage terms.

DELINQUENCY: failure of a borrower to make timely mortgage payments under a loan agreement.

DISCOUNT POINT: normally paid at closing and generally calculated to be equivalent to 1% of the total loan amount, discount points are paid to reduce the interest rate on a loan.

DOWN PAYMENT: the portion of a home's purchase price that is paid in cash and is not part of the mortgage loan.

E

EARNEST MONEY: money put down by a potential buyer to show that he or she is serious about purchasing the home; it becomes part of the down payment if the offer is accepted, is returned if the offer is rejected, or is forfeited if the buyer pulls out of the deal.

EEM: Energy Efficient Mortgage; an FHA program that helps homebuyers save money on utility bills by enabling them to finance the cost of adding energy efficiency features to a new or existing home as part of the home purchase.

EQUITY: an owner's financial interest in a property; calculated by subtracting the amount still owed on the mortgage loan(s) from the fair market value of the property.

ESCROW ACCOUNT: a separate account into which the lender puts a portion of each monthly mortgage payment; an escrow account provides the funds needed for such expenses as property taxes, homeowners insurance, mortgage insurance, etc.

F

FAIR HOUSING ACT: a law that prohibits discrimination in all facets of the home-buying process on the basis of race, color, national origin, religion, sex, familial status, or disability.

FAIR MARKET VALUE: the hypothetical price that a willing buyer and seller will agree upon when they are acting freely, carefully, and with complete knowledge of the situation.

FANNIE MAE: Federal National Mortgage Association (FNMA); a federally-chartered enterprise owned by private stockholders that purchases residential mortgages and converts them into securities for sale to investors; by purchasing mortgages, Fannie Mae supplies funds that lenders may loan to potential homebuyers.

FHA: Federal Housing Administration; established in 1934 to advance home-ownership opportunities for all Americans; assists homebuyers by providing mortgage insurance to lenders to cover most losses that may occur when a borrower defaults; this encourages lenders to make loans to borrowers who might not qualify for conventional mortgages.

FIXED-RATE MORTGAGE: a mortgage with payments that remain the same throughout the life of the loan because the interest rate and other terms are fixed and do not change.

FLOOD INSURANCE: insurance that protects homeowners against losses from a flood; if a home is located in a flood plain; the lender will require flood insurance before approving a loan.

FORECLOSURE: a legal process in which mortgaged property is sold to pay the loan of the defaulting borrower.

FREDDIE MAC: Federal Home Loan Mortgage Corporation (FHLM); a federally-chartered corporation that purchases residential mortgages, securitizes them, and sells them to investors; this provides lenders with funds for new homebuyers.

G

GINNIE MAE: Government National Mortgage Association (GNMA); a government-owned corporation overseen by the U.S. Department of Housing and Urban Development, Ginnie Mae pools FHA-insured and VA-guaranteed loans to back securities for private investment; as with Fannie Mae and Freddie Mac, the investment income provides funding that may then be lent to eligible borrowers by lenders.

GOOD FAITH ESTIMATE: an estimate of all closing fees including pre-paid and escrow items as well as lender charges; must be given to the borrower within three days after submission of a loan application.

H

HOME INSPECTION: an examination of the structure and mechanical systems to determine a home's safety; makes the potential homebuyer aware of any repairs that may be needed.

HOME WARRANTY: offers protection for mechanical systems and attached appliances against unexpected repairs not covered by homeowner's insurance; overage extends over a specific time period and does not cover the home's structure.

HOMEOWNER'S INSURANCE: an insurance policy that combines protection against damage to a dwelling and its contents with protection against claims of negligence or inappropriate action that result in someone's injury or property damage.

HUD: the U.S. Department of Housing and Urban Development; established in 1965, HUD works to create a decent home and suitable living environment for all Americans; it does this by addressing housing needs, improving and developing American communities, and enforcing fair housing laws.

HVAC: Heating, Ventilation and Air Conditioning; a home's heating and cooling system.

I

INDEX: a measurement used by lenders to determine changes to the interest rate charged on an adjustable rate mortgage.

INFLATION: the number of dollars in circulation exceeds the amount of goods and services available for purchase; inflation results in a decrease in the dollar's value.

INTEREST: a fee charged for the use of money.

INTEREST RATE: the amount of interest charged on a monthly loan payment; usually expressed as a percentage.

INSURANCE: protection against a specific loss over a period of time that is secured by the payment of a regularly scheduled premium.

J

JUDGMENT: a legal decision; when requiring debt repayment, a judgment may include a property lien that secures the creditor's claim by providing a collateral source.

L

LEASE PURCHASE: assists homebuyers in purchasing a home by allowing them to lease a home with an option to buy; the rent payment is made up of the monthly rental payment plus an additional amount that is credited to an account for use as a down payment.

LIEN: a legal claim against property that must be satisfied when the property is sold.

LOAN: money borrowed that is usually repaid with interest.

LOAN FRAUD: purposely giving incorrect information on a loan application in order to better qualify for a loan; may result in civil liability or criminal penalties.

LOAN-TO-VALUE (LTV) RATIO: a percentage calculated by dividing the amount borrowed by the price or appraised value of the home to be purchased; the higher the LTV, the less cash a borrower is required to pay as down payment.

LOCK-IN: since interest rates can change frequently, many lenders offer an interest rate lock-in that guarantees a specific interest rate if the loan is closed within a specific time.

LOSS MITIGATION: a process to avoid foreclosure; the lender tries to help a borrower who has been unable to make loan payments and is in danger of defaulting on his or her loan.

M

MARGIN: an amount the lender adds to an index to determine the interest rate on an adjustable rate mortgage.

MORTGAGE: a lien on the property that secures the promise to repay a loan.

MORTGAGE BANKER: a company that originates loans and resells them to secondary mortgage lenders like Fannie Mae or Freddie Mac.

MORTGAGE BROKER: a firm that originates and processes loans for a number of lenders.

MORTGAGE INSURANCE: a policy that protects lenders against some or most of the losses that can occur when a borrower defaults on a mortgage loan; mortgage insurance is required primarily for borrowers with a down payment of less than 20% of the home's purchase price.

MORTGAGE INSURANCE PREMIUM (MIP): a monthly payment – usually part of the mortgage payment – paid by a borrower for mortgage insurance.

MORTGAGE MODIFICATION: a loss mitigation option that allows a borrower to refinance and/or extend the term of the mortgage loan and thus reduce the monthly payments.

O

OFFER: indication by a potential buyer of a willingness to purchase a home at a specific price; generally put forth in writing.

ORIGINATION: the process of preparing, submitting, and evaluating a loan application; generally includes a credit check, verification of employment, and a property appraisal.

ORIGINATION FEE: the charge for originating a loan; is usually calculated in the form of points and paid at closing.

P

PARTIAL CLAIM: a loss mitigation option offered by the FHA that allows a borrower, with help from a lender, to get an interest-free loan from HUD to bring their mortgage payments up to date.

PITI: Principal, Interest, Taxes, and Insurance – the four elements of a monthly mortgage payment; payments of principal and interest go directly toward repaying the loan while the portion that covers taxes and insurance (homeowner's and mortgage, if applicable) goes into an escrow account to cover the fees when they are due.

PMI: Private Mortgage Insurance; privately-owned companies that offer standard and special affordable mortgage insurance programs for qualified borrowers with down payments of less than 20% of a purchase price.

PRE-APPROVE: lender commits to lend to a potential borrower; commitment remains as long as the borrower still meets the qualification requirements at the time of purchase.

PRE-FORECLOSURE SALE: allows a defaulting borrower to sell the mortgaged property to satisfy the loan and avoid foreclosure.

PRE-QUALIFY: a lender informally determines the maximum amount an individual is eligible to borrow.

PREMIUM: an amount paid on a regular schedule by a policyholder that maintains insurance coverage.

PREPAYMENT: payment of the mortgage loan before the scheduled due date; may be subject to a prepayment penalty.

PRINCIPAL: the amount borrowed from a lender; doesn't include interest or additional fees.

R

RADON: a radioactive gas found in some homes that, if occurring in strong enough concentrations, can cause health problems.

REAL ESTATE AGENT: an individual who is licensed to negotiate and arrange real estate sales; works for a real estate broker.

REALTOR: a real estate agent or broker who is a member of the NATIONAL ASSOCIATION OF REALTORS, and its local and state associations.

REFINANCING: paying off one loan by obtaining another; refinancing is generally done to secure better loan terms (like a lower interest rate).

REHABILITATION MORTGAGE: a mortgage that covers the costs of rehabilitating (repairing or improving) a property; some rehabilitation mortgages – like the FHA's 203(k) – allow a borrower to roll the costs of rehabilitation and home purchase into one mortgage loan.

RESPA: Real Estate Settlement Procedures Act; a law protecting consumers from abuses during the residential real estate purchase and loan process by requiring lenders to disclose all settlement costs, practices, and relationships.

S

SETTLEMENT: another name for closing.

SPECIAL FORBEARANCE: a loss mitigation option where the lender arranges a revised repayment plan for the borrower that may include a temporary reduction or suspension of monthly loan payments.

SUBORDINATE: to place in a rank of lesser importance or to make one claim secondary to another.

SURVEY: a property diagram that indicates legal boundaries, easements, encroachments, rights of way, improvement locations, etc.

SWEAT EQUITY: using labor to build or improve a property as part of the down payment.

T

TITLE 1: an FHA-insured loan that allows a borrower to make non-luxury improvements (like renovations or repairs) to their home; Title I loans less than $7,500 don't require a property lien.

TITLE INSURANCE: insurance that protects the lender against any claims that arise from arguments about ownership of the property; also available for homebuyers.

TITLE SEARCH: a check of public records to be sure that the seller is the recognized owner of the real estate and that there are no unsettled liens or other claims against the property.

TRUTH-IN-LENDING: a federal law obligating a lender to give full written disclosure of all fees, terms, and conditions associated with the loan initial period and then adjusts to another rate that lasts for the term of the loan.

UNDERWRITING: the process of analyzing a loan application to determine the amount of risk involved in making the loan; it includes a review of the potential borrower's credit history and a judgment of the property value.

VA: Department of Veterans Affairs: a federal agency which guarantees loans made to veterans; similar to mortgage insurance, a loan guarantee protects lenders against loss that may result from a borrower default.

FROM THE REALTOR'S BOOKSHELF -
RECOMMENDED REAL ESTATE READING

Although I've designed this book so that it's your one-shop-stop for all things buying and selling a home – and even working with a realtor – I know that I haven't included every tip, tactic, pie chart or graph.

To further your education,
I've included below a list of helpful real estate books.
The Millionaire Real Estate Investor by Gary Keller
(Simon & Schuster Publishing Co., 2004)
How to List & Sell Real Estate by Danielle Kennedy
(Simon & Schuster, 1983)
Investing in Fixer-Uppers by Jay P. DeCima
(McGraw-Hill, 2003)

ACKNOWLEDGEMENTS

DAVID NORDLUND (COVER GRAPHICS) - a renowned graphics designer in Los Angeles whose work has been widely recognized in the entertainment industry. He has worked on projects that have received Academy Awards. His work has been showcased in many major motion pictures and Fortune 500 Corporations. A friend and an incredibly talented individual.
www.TenthPlanetAdv.com

RUSSELL BAER (COVER PHOTO) – a prominent photographer in Los Angeles with a flair for making all of his clients look and feel like a celebrity…at least for a day. A truly amazing talent who has grown exponentially in his craft over the past few years.
www.RussellBaer.com

LUANNE IANNUCCI - a preeminent hair designer and makeup artist in the Beverly Hills and Hollywood area. Her amazing talent, warmth and positive energy make her a delight to work with.
Amato Salon in Beverly Hills

RUSTY FISCHER – an Editor whose talents are beyond measure.

KAREN BOATWRIGHT – Virtual Assistant. There is nothing virtual about her. She is always ready to help day or night. Although she lives 2000 miles away, we work as though we are officemates. A whiz at Excel, MS Word and just about every other software package out there.
E-mail: **wvteardrop@gmail.com**

- DISCLAIMER -

This publication is intended to provide accurate and authoritative information with regard to the subject matter covered. It is offered with the understanding that the author is not engaged in rendering legal, tax or other professional services. If legal, tax or other expert assistance is required, the services of a competent professional should be sought.

Every effort has been made to make this book as complete and accurate as possible. However, there may be mistakes, both typographical and in content. Therefore, this book should be used as a general guide and not as the ultimate resource for buying and selling real estate. Information contained herein has been carefully gathered from sources believed to be reliable.

The purpose of this book is to educate and entertain. The author shall have neither liability nor responsibility to any person or entity with respect to any loss or damage caused or alleged to have been caused, directly or indirectly, by the information contained in this book.

NOTES – PAGE 1

NOTES – PAGE 2

NOTES – PAGE 3